A Littl

Joseph S. Fusaro

Foreword

Joe and I first connected during the summer of 2015 when his gorgeous photos of clouds, sunsets and mountain landscapes coupled with sincere words threaded together into verse caught my eye on Instagram.

The way Joe began to share his story through beautiful images and his simple, yet stunning rhythmic poetry, told me he was someone special. It was obvious he was putting himself out there because he knew sharing his story had the power to save a life. I'd later find out that when Joe's mental illness stole everything from him, he was searching for a sign that things could get better. The same way I sought out positive stories of recovery when I was at my lowest point struggling with my bipolar disorder.

When I realized Joe lived in New York, I knew we needed his voice for our NYC production of This Is

My Brave. My non-profit is made up of brave individuals who audition and are chosen to share their stories of overcoming mental illness through poetry, essay, and original music. Joe's artistry with words was an ideal fit for our show, so I reached out to him and encouraged him to audition. I wasn't surprised to hear weeks later that he'd made the cast, and I was thrilled I'd have to chance to meet him in person the weekend of the show.

Through his touching poem about finding the courage to share his story, Joe read about how he shifted his mindset from negative to positive in order to climb out of his darkness. His vulnerable performance will forever be etched in my memory and will no doubt inspire many, many people to seek help and know that they can get better.

Joe's poetry, at first glance, is minimalistic. But one doesn't need to compose dramatic, lengthy stanzas in order to make a lasting impact on the reader. This collection of heartfelt poems provides hope for the lost, instills a sense of belonging in those who have fallen out of touch with loved ones, and most of all, reminds us that love always wins. It's the bright star someone out there is searching for in the midst of their darkness. And I know they'll find comfort within these pages.

Jennifer Marshall
Co-Founder This Is My Brave

A Note from the Author

I fought with myself the last three years about how to present my struggle with mental illness. I have written songs. I have written scripts in the form of drama, comedy, and even an attempt at borderline fiction. I have tried to put together a documentary. My main issue has been that the story is so vast. There could be one story for all 13 years of my struggle. Those 13 years can be broken down into 13 different stories. Those thirteen stories could be broken into different scripts for each week and so on. Hell, I have had minutes that I could write a 2 hour movie about.

I recently read a story about a sailor that was lost at sea for 14 months and it took him more than 40 interviews to put the story together. With each interview he would piece it together like a puzzle. Every time he stated something new the previous parts of his story would make a little more sense. I feel like I am still in that process as my body and brain are still healing from the more than a decade of stress and neglect.

As I would start to get deep into any of these other writing projects I would always feel this pull back to poetry. Poetry is the one consistent thing I have had in my life since my teens. It has served as a timeline, therapy, and sort of like a religion during a time where I thought I had no beliefs. It would force me to evaluate my choices, set goals, and help me fix things that I was doing wrong.

I feel that poetry is art and writing in its purest form. There is something about a person, a pen, and their notebook where everything seems to unfold so naturally and honestly. There is no music or sound to sway our emotions. There is no need to give explicit or extrinsic details. Each line, feeling, or emotion can speak for itself. You do not have to relate to a whole story. We have not all been through the same situations; however we have all felt similar feelings. I am not discounting any other medium, but I feel for my first publication this was the only method I would still feel good about 25 or 50 years down the road. And who knows, perhaps longer.

I decided that for my first publication I would focus on my growth. Sure I could have spent pages talking about how some of the mental health institutions have *not been updated or refurbished since the 1960's. I could have spoken about how Doctors and nurses that have been there 20 or 30 years have never taken a refresher course to keep up with medications, new publications of the DSM, or new natural methods of healing. I could talk about how I went in to detox off of 1 or 2 medications and would leave the hospital with 6 prescriptions. I could maybe go on and on about how it took me 3 days to get a prescription for a daily vitamin during an inpatient stay. I could talk about the wet burger and fries with a sugar drink for lunch and dinner that probably did not speed up the healing process. If I really wanted to be a pain I would complain about how it took until my 7th or 8th inpatient psych stay to be told I may qualify for disability. Then there is the fact that Social Security* *payments are not enough for someone with any illness to afford a studio apartment in a damp basement on the wrong side of town. I often wonder what most of the population would do if I gave them $31 a day and said "Okay, now you must spend $50 for each doctor copayment, figure out how to eat healthy enough to heal, pay for your medications, rent, bills, clothes, transportation, or have any kind of social life. And by the way, God speed kid..." I honestly could not even imagine what I would have done had I been married with children. Because you are disabled, does NOT mean you should not leave your house, find love, have a family, or enjoy the other parts of your life. Before I forget, there was the fact (I promise there will be no more 'facts' after this) that the county and town I live in cut funding for a crisis intervention team. This* *means there are only 2 ways to get to a hospital; 1.) The back of a police car, or 2.) Get restrained, strapped to a gurney, and brought via ambulance. Either method hardly gives someone the strength or incentive to make the changes they need to in order to get better. The experience actually broke me down to nothing every time. Ah, digressions... I am forever grateful I could eat while I was sick.*

I will not complain because somehow I made it through the psychological maze that gets put in front of someone that is already at one of the saddest and most difficult points of their life.

I will use this book, this platform, to briefly touch upon 2008 when I first hit rock bottom. I had just lost my home, relationship, job, possessions, family, and friends. I was hardly on par with all of my peers that had just finished college, had new jobs, or fancy new cars. I assumed they would use their weekends to check the housing market during the day. Then go to the bar at night to talk to women about their new car and what houses they were interested in. On the other hand, I had just gotten out of an inpatient stay at a mental hospital that was like taking a trip back to the early 1900's in terms of aesthetics and medicine. I had never been so terrified in my life. The scary thing about being in a mental hospital is that when you start to show concern or fear for your well-being they diagnose you with paranoia and just add more medication or extend your stay. And please do not rely too heavily on sarcasm and overreacting as this will most definitely push you into the 'schizo' realm of diagnoses. I need to note; this is all easy for me to say as I look back but I often wonder if knowing to relax would have made any difference for me at the time or if I was so deep into mania that I really could not control myself. It is probably a little bit of both.

Fortunately, and unfortunately I was raised a fighter. No not physically, but I was taught that if I feel that I am being misled or cheated in any way that I should stand up for my beliefs no matter what. It took me until 2013 to learn to 1.) Keep my mouth shut unless it was for breathing, and 2.) Life was not about fighting; it was about redirecting your negative energy into something that is positive. We all go through some kind of difficult time in our lives. We must learn from the difficult times. It is not about what we went through. It is about how we can help the next person so that it is a little bit easier for them.

After I briefly touch upon the 5 years I spent at rock bottom, I focus on my crawl back into reality between 2014 and 2015. When I was engulfed in my worst depression episodes or flying alongside mania, I could not find light. I could not find light in the people I met, which I think was because I did not give off any light. I could not find light on television. I could not find light on the radio. I could not find light in the newspaper, and honestly I was far too overwhelmed to pick out a book and way too dyslexic to read it. I needed to create my own light. It took a few positive swipes of a pen, a couple prayers, an almost dry drop of hope, and some momentum in the right direction. I was able to find a little light, take a breath, and find a little more time.

I really hope you enjoy this and I do not mean that you are entertained. Rather that you see that there is hope after agoraphobia, depression, bipolar, schizophrenia, borderline, etcetera. I recommend that you share it with anyone you know that is suffering with serious mental health issues. 12% of the profit from this book will be going to the mental health organization This Is My Brave that gave me strength, confidence, support, and so much more by teaching me to use my story to help others feel less alone. Their mottos of "Be brave" and "Storytelling saves lives" could not be truer and I thank them from the bottom of my heart for opening me up to a better place and a better life for those of us with mental illness.

10 Years (Lost)

I am fucking out of here. I love this. I hate it. It has been too long. Sell your guitar. I cannot deal with anyone. I am overwhelmed. 6 dollars, for a pack of cigarettes? Make an appointment. This is the place. I am free. I am going to be a mess later. It is so late. I am not tired. Economics. It has been too long. We are staying up again tonight. I cannot take her anymore. I am done. I am back. I am done. This time I am really done. It has been too long. Wasted time. I have not slept in months. It does not matter. Make an appointment. Business major. Did you call your friend for me? Write it down. I need a job. Work is boring. Pick up your guitar. It has been too long. She would be great. 7 dollars, for a pack of cigarettes? The timing is not right. Write it down. It has been too long. Do you remember? This alarm. I think I got 2 hours of sleep last night. I hate my job. Did you call your friend for me? The days feel so long. When did everything get so heavy? That was a song. I cannot take it anymore. I am so nauseous. Make an appointment. I think I want to go back to college. Astronomy. I need to leave town. Write it down. Replay that album. Learn that song. Write your own. It sounds just like that one from 1991. Write it down. Apply for a new job. Scratch it out. Sleep. I think it has been a month. A week? Felt like. Make an appointment. It has been too long. This is the place. I finally feel free. I finally feel home. 8 dollars, for a pack of cigarettes? I am having trouble reading. I cannot wake up. Place some bets. Philosophy. Go for a run. I am fine. Make an appointment. Get a job. What about home? I am getting really sick. Did you call your friend for me? Write it down. Find a guitar. It is too much. I cannot kick this cough. Buy more cigarettes. How much does it pay? Play another song. Sleep it off. I am so cold. It is summer. This cough. Smoke it off. It is not in my head. I need a medical doctor. It is all in your head. Here is something for the cough however I am pretty sure the problem is in your head not your lung. 9 dollars, for a pack of cigarettes? Make a new appointment. Sleep through it. There is no such thing as…no. Sleep it off. I have not slept in months. I need to go home. I have no way to explain this. I need to go home. My stomach. You need an appointment. I need a promotion. Relax, I am going. I need a job. I need money. I am a little tired. I am confused and sick. You need to do something. Write another song. I need a new home. I need money. I need to catch up. I love being home. Make an appointment. Not there. I guess this is home. 10 dollars, for a pack of cigarettes? Keep up with that job. I need something that will help me stay awake. Not this again. Everything is going to work out great. Write it down. I have not slept in days. Make an appointment. I cannot take that. It makes me sleep. I am too busy. I need to move up. I need to keep up. I need to make more money. 11 dollars, for a pack of cigarettes? I need to stop. This is all crazy. Everyone else is definitely crazy. Call an ex. Write it down. I have not slept…

YOU HAVE NOT SLEPT IN YEARS. YOU NEED TO REEVAULATE EVERYTHING. YOU NEED TO STOP. YOU NEED TO RELEARN THE PROPER WAY TO THINK. You need to, this is really hard, but we need to take you in.

But wait! I am not angry. I am not crazy. I was just being… I was so broken and needed to get lifted. I could not find it physically and these pills couldn't do it. I am paying some guy to be my friend once a month while everyone looks on waiting for something to come of it. I just *sleep*

There goes

Another month.

Speechless 08

Infinite crystals
Bright lit up trucks
My next love found skating
On glass in a park

Bare oak
With white sparks

This city is just

Listen
Just listen

The city
The desert
The woods
The beach

FUCK THE WEATHER

Which city can I trust

Rely on Love

Always our mission
Flakes in Hollywood glisten

So fly

High

And stay

Hush

When I am with you at the end of this rush

My family
I left them
My only gift
Is your touch

Last hour of Christmas
Pine fades into dark

Did I neglect to mention
I beat with your heart

Did I forget to notice
We will be too far apart

If Saint Which
Leaves me you

Wrapped tight on my bow
I'll sharpen this arrow
Pierce between my eyes
A thought frozen in snow

Where am I
That is not you
Where did they all go
This doesn't feel home

THIS IS NOT MY FUCKING HOME

I pretend to pray
To one day have a dream
I can hate them to show

Do not take for granted
The ones that grew cold

So this line is over
Evolution of our life
Our life together

Maybe?
Starts?

Did I mention to mention
I beat with your heart

Did I mention to mention
I beat in your heart

Did I forget to mention
I beat with your heart

Did I mention to mention
This is too hard

24 December 2008 (4:27am)

He Said (You're Far Too Gone)

Again
It. won't. be. long.
But your. way. too. far. to make it

It's way too long
And you're far too gone to make it

I told you son
If they find out they will break you

If you hold on strong
We can send someone to save you

He said
You've come so far
But you still got Time don’t waste it

You were gone so long
And we didn't think you'd make it

You were gone so long
And we never thought you'd make it

You were gone so long
And we didn't think you'd make it

He said
If you just ask son
We can find a way to raze you

It's the same damn song
I've been singing since the 80's

If you say too much
We will send someone to break you

If you lived this long
Nothing will ever take you

Winter 2010

SzAD (Lyrics)

Hey all
How long
You took the time to cure it all
How long?
And I don't
I don't think I can take
It anymore

How long
How long
You took the time to cure it all
How long?
And I don't
I don't think I can take
You anymore

This time I thought I saw you
Coming back
Coming back
Coming back

This time I thought I saw you
Coming back
Coming back
Coming back

This time I thought I saw you
Coming back
Coming back
Coming home

Home (echo)

Been down and broken hearted
I will carry you home
On the ground is where I started
I will carry you home
Spent all my love on money
I will carry you home

Home (echo)

If you feel like talking to heaven
If you feel like coming home
If you feel
Like walking to heaven
You're gonna walk alone
You're gonna walk alone

I do not have an exact date, but 'SzAD' was one of the few things I wrote between 2010 and 2012 due to the side effects of my medication. This was the least I had written in my life.

Fucked up

Why does everything get all fucked up
When I decide to try
I wanted so bad just to sleep
For the rest of my life

I'd take 28 pills
Just enough
To buy me some time

Although the warning on the bottle read

"Whatever you do,
Just don't take 29"

Ironic shit that happens when
You are scared as hell to die

Get some rest
No I mean some real deal
2 to 3 years of hibernation

You are far too addicted to concentration

The revelations

You can't even get that right

What now Genius?

Mass elation

Don't worry
Don't think
Don't love
Don't lust

Find help
Find light
Find warmth
Find trust

20,000 pills later
I got an Rx for a hug

Now go
Make up with your old friend

I missed you
I thought about you often
I know I should have said
I thought that was what I sent you
In the letter you read

Ah yes

My body was working
While my soul was dead

I am not about to get into this again.

But I was never mad

The end

The Moral of the Story

god
bless
equal
sum
peace
love
all
one

Dream All Night

Dream of me
Dream tonight
Dream on TV
Dream all night

Dream to cleanse
Dream in rhyme
Dream of you
Dream all night

Dream I cannot reach
Dream I do not have time
Dream of me
Dream all night

Dream half a story
Dream truth into lies
Dream of you
Dream all night

Dream I am sliding
Dream I can fly
Dream of me
Dream all night

Dream of my death
Dream about life
Dream of you
Dream all night

Dream out of focus
Dream I'm not right
Dream of me
Dream all night

Dream about love
Dream there is no time
Dream of you
Dream all night

Dream understand me
Dream deep inside
Dream of me
Dream all night

Dream ‘til I'm with you
Dream ‘til you are mine
Dream of you and me
Dream until the end of time

Wake up alone
It is okay
I am alright

Can we continue that dream?

Please God
Just try

2013 (2:58am)

Magic Little Seed

Looking at my tree

Little branch

Little stem

Little bud

Little flower

Little Leaves

If we are ever so lucky

We may find some seeds

All your crazy roots

Juiced up on electricity

Amazing tree

A friend to me

With your help

I will learn to see

All the benefits

Of planting that seed

2013

Seen it All *into* Always on My Mind

We're seeing it all

We've seen it all

We've seen it all

We've seen it all

We're seeing it
all over again

We're seeing it
all over again

We're seeing it all

We've seen it all

We've seen it all

We've seen it all

We're seeing it
all over again

We're seeing it
all over again

La la la la

La la la la la la la la
La la la la la la la la
La la la la la la la la

Don't want to live
Don't want to die

We're here to celebrate our time
Those stars are always on my mind
Those stars are always on my mind

Burn down your troubles
Read a sign

We're gonna wake you in the night
Those stars are always on my mind

Those stars are always on my mind

If I should hold you
To the light

Write me a letter to the sky
Those stars are always on my mind
Those stars are always on my mind

And when I wake up
Hold me tight

Help me straighten out my life
Those stars are always on my mind
Those stars are always on my mind

Shake up your eyes
Feel the shine

Of Diamond lights bright in the sky
Those stars are always on my mind
Those stars are always on my mind

And if they wake you
In the night

Just write the song You'll be alright
Those stars are always on my mind

Those stars are always on my mind

If you give me
one more try

I swear to everything that's right
Those stars are always on my mind
Those stars are always on my mind

If you're feeling
color blind

Can't find the light can't make a dime
Those stars are always on my mind
Those stars are always on my mind

You start to think
You're still alive

They say a job will save your life
Those stars are always on my mind
Those stars are always on my mind

And if I fuck up
One more time

Make sure you blame me 'til I die
Those stars are always on my mind

Those stars are always on my mind

Write your story
Hold a sign

Fuck! Do something with my life
Those stars are always on my mind
Those stars are always on my mind

La la   la la
La la   la la

La la   la la   la la la la
La la   la la   la la la la
La la   la la   la la la la

La la   la la
La la   la la

La la   la la   la la la la
La la   la la   la la la la
La la   la la   la la la la

?oseph S. Fusaro (June 2013)

Who Knows? (Lyrics)

Who knows why we wait so long
Who knows why we wait so long
Who knows why i wrote this song

And I can't give
My time away

Who knows why we wait so long
Who knows why we wait so long
Who knows why I can’t move on

And I can't save
The time I waste

Who knows why we wait so long
Who knows why we wait so long
Who knows how we got so strong

And I can't leave
But I can't stay

Who knows

Why I wrote this song

27 June 2013 (2am)

Searching For a Path

I've been searching for a path
A path with just solutions

I've been looking for a path

The one without delusion

The one that is not an illusion

The One

Without conclusions

(August 2013)

Midnight (Loose Associations)

Midnight
Late Show
All the stars
Shine like snow

Breathe In
Your nose
What time is it
Please take me home

They say my
Aura Glows
Find a map
Dry my clothes

Repeat
Favorite Show
Light the fuse
Watch her know

Morning glory
Wake me
Shake the cherries
Out of my tree

John Walker
Apple Seeds
Take my money
Let me be

Take my time
Let me be
Take my lover
Let me be

Take my home
Let me be
Take my family
Let me be

Take my friends
Let me be
Purgatory
Far from free

My Dearest Midnight
It's half past Three

31 October 2013

Alone I Wait

Alone I wait
For my soul to escape
For my mind to be free
For my body to heal
This cannot be real

Alone I wait
For the flowers to grow
For the brook to rise
From the melting of snow
I cannot wait to go

Alone I wait
For the silence of night
For the people to understand
For the answers we fight
I do not have the time

Alone I wait
For the day I can love
For the day I can run
For the ability to fly above
There is no line; Don't push & shove

8 November 2013

Mother Nature Father Time

We watch the clock
We pray for time

We look for love
We pick a side

We walk through the maze
We cut the line

We work for nothing
We never lie

The streets are empty
Turn off the light

We think about sleep
We don't feel alright

We listen to music
We don't mind

We feed our children
We stay up all night

We climb a tree
We look up at the sky

All of my fears
No compromise

Slip into my dreams
Wash my poor mind

I pray for you

Mother Nature
Father Time

We stare at what is different
We feel better inside

We chop cherry trees
We keep saying like

We fly into the sun
We begin to go blind

We watch life in a box
We go for a drive

This is my life
So psick but so kind

We beg on the streets
We put wheels on a bike

We look into the camera
We always cross eyes

We scratch our new records
We say we don't mind

We blast mountains for gravel
We laugh while some cry

Something inside me
Just needs to die

Will you continue to love me
Please give me a sign

I pray for you

Mother Nature
Father Time

January 2014

Back For More (Lyrics)

Intro

A heart beats in everyone
I know
Just saying
Welcome to the show

And I can't sleep
And weeee can't breathe

The time your body washed up
Onto shore
You couldn't swim
No more

And I want to scream
God help us please

I fucked up everything
You know
Wouldn’t you know she's coming
Back for more

And I wanted to fly
Before we die

I've fucked up everything
& sold
All the love & now
I must go

Find another way and you'll get in
Another record I'll be there

A heart beats in everyone
I know
Just saying welcome to
The show

And I can't sleep
And weeee can't breathe

I think I'll take this tunnel
Back to home
God gives us words to
Let you know

That I'm a freak
Can you please press release

Breathe

Ahhhhhhh

13 May 2014

Couldn't Anymore (Lyrics)

I've been

Alone and daydreaming

And it's come

In time for the season

And I feel

That I can't come fake with it

And I can't take the heat

Anymore

I've seen

Her begging and dealing

But I still

Let her eyes deceive me

As my thoughtsthoughtsthoughts

Start freezing up

Now I'm tired of the cold

As you know

She takes

Pictures of only us

And gives

Strangers

Film they develop

Erase them

And I couldn't see you

And I cannot stay here

Anymore

August 2014

Align

The space
The wait
The weight
The weights
To give
With no hate
To feel
All the love
A place where
We can look up
Romantic
With lust
To awake
With no fear
To awake
With you near
To awake
My old tears
To inflate
My own mind
Only beauty
And time
To escape from
The pain

Feel relief
Once again

And this
Will never
End

Because that is what Infinity said...

26 September 2014

Blue Moon (Full Circle)

A dissipating storm
End the war
End the war

Tell them where you are from
Start the fun
Start the fun

Release all of your hate
It's not too late
It is not too late

Repair my lonely mind
So much time
So much time

Let us feel the love
Not just one
Every one

Blue moon rocks
Fall again
Onto my friend
My only friend

The wrong substance for pain
It was all the same
They were all the same

Something I should have said

I do not know if I ever really wished
I were dead

It was more like
Goodbye for right now and I will

See you in a
Couple of days

With a

Fresh head

End the hurt once again

There is no end?

All bad things end

Write down how you really feel
Then push send

5 November 2014 (Edited 1 August 2015)

Sunday Morning

Sunday morning

Record playing

All the things

I am not saying

Because I found

A peace of mind

Today I only

Have some time

To rest my head

To calm my life

Have no concerns

No hate

No vice

No time

To think about

My good times passed

This day is going

Way too fast

Oh yes Sunday

You should last

8 November 2014 (2:15am)

Getting Old

I am only happy
When you love me

I wonder if
One day you might be

I send a letter
To the world

I love that girl

No

I love this girl

I am quite content
Enough to stress

I am so tired
My mind cannot rest

If I could have all
The diamonds in this world

I would take that girl

No.

I will take this girl

Every time
A device rings

Every word
The singer sings

I think about you
Every night

They say you are...
But what is life?

Without the heat
Without a soul

Oh, my God;

I am getting old.

9 November 2014. (6:29pm)

Inflation

Your
Love

Your
Prayer

Your
Sympathy

Means more
To me

Than

Your
Money

10 November 2014 (2:33pm)

Dear Dear Young Writer

The eldest of songs
Will be new to someone
There is still time
The line is long
There is a way
To live up
To the bar that they set
Though I can't reach it yet
I reach up once more
And I will reach up each morning
Until I can stretch
Until the sky
Never ends
Until this fire sets
Putting my mind at rest

It is over

The test

God Speed

Kindness and concern

Are lethal to negativity

I got me

From here on out

Wish me

God speed

It is all I need

It is all I need

7 December 2014 (11:30pm)

Hours Inside Of Minutes

There's no switch in this hall
And all the lights are off
Oh my God I am fucked up
Oh my God I am in love
I have work in the morning
What was twilights warning
This writing's so boring
I must be alone
You say I cannot be fun

I have so many things to do when I wake
I think it is wise to set my alarm for 8

No wait

7:45

That's not going to work

7:42

Nope

7:51

Perfect

That is going to make it much easier to sleep

Take this song off repeat

Gravity only knows my feet

Repeat

Repeat

Shuffle

Buffle

Noobles on a plate

I will take a baker's dozen

That is 13 noobles

Damn kid behind the fucking counter

Only gave me 8

Ride the sound wave

Reflect the ultraviolet rays

Your son has set

His minds cooled off

Later on

We need to talk

Oh fuck

Do not leave

We love you

But you are a bit abrupt

A little love

A little love

What the fuck is the name of that song?

Had to be Elvis

The Beatles

Or nope

Who knows

Could be Larry Gobert

And the Dirty Used Easels

I am starting to look at the world from afar

My macro 3rd eye

Chakra's in style

Do not eat after 6

Wait make that 5

Stay a while

Come inside

Who sang that song?

Dave, Bob, and Jimi

Are all on my mind

The story continues

There is still so much time

Age

We age

I keep wondering if I should send you this page

22 December 2014 (10:55pm)

Another Opinion

Eccentric
Esoteric

Must be my
Indisposition

When how where

Will I

Finally

Learn to listen

31 December 2014

A New Year

I awake

I think

I am on earth

The beat starts up

And the first song was sung

I bet you everything in the world

The only feeling was love

1 January 2015

Nerves

Fruit is the fuel

Water is the solvent

Air keeps me light

And my mind takes care of all of it

My senses keep things real

My nerves make me feel

Our emotions spin the wheel

Hi

I am trying to be me

What is your deal?

2 January 2015

Alone At Night

I do not want to go to bed alone anymore.

I am so cold at night and I shiver ‘til morning

God if you hear me please send me some warming

I think I can love the next girl with a heart

I think I need someone now

Because tomorrow is too far

Please just

Overnight me

A shooting star

10 January 2015 (2:25am)

Crazy

I love you
I love you

I'm crazy

I love you

13 January 2015 (2:34am)

The Wait

The whole
Time

We were
Only
Waiting

For

Ourselves

January 2015

A Mile

Here comes the sun

Watch all the souls run

Yearning to fly

There is infinite time

There is infinite sky

Distance from the light

Can't be much more

Than a mile

By the way

I love your style

16 January 2015

Apple

So what you are telling me

Is that that red ball grows on this tree

And this tree grew from that apple's great great great great grandfathers seed

Every year
More and more apples
And more and more trees
And they are all for you
And along the way
I can take some for me
These plants are perfect
These apples are free

Thank you apple
Thank you nature
Thank you stem
Thank you bud
Thank you roots
Thank you dirt
Thank you friends
Thank you water
Thank you sun
Thank you seed

Thank you leaf
Thank you tree

Really?
Are you serious?

Yes!

These apples are free.

19 January 2015 (9:53)

The Persistence of Passion

Sincerely
I start

I am using
My heart

I am wishing
On stars

Am I thinking
Too hard

Hurry
Please
Get in the car

Look
Over there

I see the light
It is not far

22 January 2015

Snow (Juno)

I want to burrow myself into peace
I want to bury my heart in love

I want to live long
What?
It sounds fun.

I do not want to go home
I am covered in snow

Brrrrr...

Now I am cold.

Another note
Another song
Another cup of tea
Perhaps a good read
Then we move on

28 January 2015

I Lost a Friend

She always had a place for me

She always had a smiling face for me

She opened her arms to help raise me

She taught me how to read through all the world's mess

She taught me to not give a damn about life's stress

Although at this moment I am cold and sad

I am reminded you are the best friend our family has ever had

5 February 2015 (10:00am)

Love II

I was searching
Far too wide
For the world
The first 30 years of my life

Then an awakening
Perhaps just todays realization

Not one more question
Not a doubt in my mind

I repeat

If I keep my energy focused
If I keep my heart true

What?
What is next?
What should I do?

Breathe
It is ok

The world will start to look for you

9 February 2015

Rain

It is a new day
We treat Paper
In the strangest way
I wonder if she will stay?

You know
My message is not only ironic
But it is screaming CLICHÉ

Purchase your review?

Follow me
Brick Shoes

Into the lake

Selfie
Selfie
You better not fucking H8

I cannot relate
I will not relate
I need to relate

One day…

Unfulfilled
They took you off top bill

I have nothing left

Here

Take this

It is my name

You know

You need my product
For this low low price

In fact
I will make it
2 for 1
For you
Today

Fuck it man
Buy as many as you can take

$hit

I have sold all of my umbrellas
and it has just begun to rain

February 2015 (late)

Sheep

I pray to be conscious of my mistakes

I meditate to maybe change my ways

I pray to sleep in peace each night

I meditate that one day we all see the light

I pray for my family

I pray they are happy

I meditate every day

I will find better ways

I pray to respect each person I meet

I meditate away defiance as it makes me weak

I pray that my friends all keep love in their soul

I meditate for my lover so that I can give her it all

I pray for this nature

I pray for our sky

I pray for just a sip of water

I pray for the earth

I pray for more time

I am counting some sheep

And they are counting on me

To get it right.

Off to dream

Bye bye

9 February 2015

Feeding

It is okay
If someone else says it better

Just another reason
We are all in this together

18 February 2015

Exhaustion

I
Can
Not
Feel

For

Every
One

Anymore

17 February 2015

Never ever

Negative
Will never
Flow through
Me

Again

18 February 2015 (12:07am)

DX

Avolition
Anhedonia
Satirical misrepresentation
They stole it from her

SzAD SzAD SzAD
And a little bipolar

That is my girl
They misdiagnosed her

This is my girl
My amazing lover
My only one
I use my time just to show her

20 February 2015 (2:28pm)

Push Pull

Magnet to my heat
The light that rises

Wakes my mind

Magnet to my body
Addicted to my mouth

She is the Queen of New York
But she was raised in the south

24 February 2015 (7:48pm)

Faith in Me

I am done hoping all of my days away

I spent the last few years hoping
What a mistake

Now I get it

If it was not meant to be
She is not going to stay

They shout:

We want this
We want that

We

CAN

NOT

Wait

Patience
Structure
Healthy ways
A little educate

Put the issue to rest

It is time for us
It is time for trust

This morning I will look up the definition of faith.

24 February 2015 (7:00am)

Ordinary Day

I will cry for loss

I will cry for gain

I will not cry!
On an ordinary day

I will then...

Cry again.

I will cry because I am full

I will cry when I am past empty

I will not cry!
Out in profanity

I will always...

Cry for sanity.

Angelica

Bite your tongue
Fight the thought

Take the time to
Read it all

It is just the
Re-presentation

Of an old
Declaration

I think I have
Heard this song

In that case
It won't be long

For a new state of
Over anxious elation

Because the citizens
Are waiting

And no one has
Been bathing

The scent is
Resonating

And our DNA's
Gone crazy

We think so much
That we are lazy

Then the real world
Gets hazy

I think it is time
At least maybe

Regular people
are going to hate me

I wonder what
Will they name me

On the cover
Of the paper

Did you read this
They saved her

Denomination
Numerator

The extra

Remainder

I think her
I will take her

Please write
What you need
Or her name
On this paper

Okay then,

Peace
Love
&
Angelica Savior

Winter 2014-2015

There is no greater light than her smile in my eyes.

February Nights

Finally do yourself
A favor

Sit back to write today

Are my words
Necessary

Do not place any blame

See the world's
encouragement

Clean up the
Last little pieces

And make sure you save the frame

There is always
A new piece of glass

And new photographs will come your way

February 2015 (9:12pm)

Mess

Some
flight
Some
fight
Some
figure it out

Some
laugh
Some
sigh
Some
speak with their eyes

Some
hate
Some
obsess
We keep
Cleaning your mess

I REPEAT
I REPEAT

WE KEEP
CLEANING YOUR MESS

Some
see

Some
feel

Some of us know

When it is real

1 March 2015

O's

The wind begins to
Blow
Blow
Blow

I am a little
Cold
Cold
Cold

I need a little
Soul
Soul
Soul

I feel a little
Old
Old
Old

I wish I could
Go
Go
Go

Do you even
Know
Know
Know

My mind feels a little
Slow
Slow
Slow

My coffee is growing
Mold
Mold
Mold

Her phone is on airplane
Mode
Mode
Mode

I wish I could reconfigure the
Code
Code
Code

The thieves keep yelling
Sold
Sold
Sold

Another hand dealt, I learn to
Fold
Fold
Fold

3 March 2015 (Midnight)

Sunday Morning II

Learn something new with each day

Another cliché they may say

But if I am still awake

But if I could find a way

Quiet please
It is Sunday

Winter 2015

Another Long Drawn Out Goodbye

Kindness and concern
Are lethal to negativity

Please do not judge

Maybe

Help

Me

If you refuse to do that

At least wish me

God speed…

Please

Peace

Zero

Zero games
No wasted time
The world is ours
This piece is mine

All sweat
All heart
All tears
Some scars
That are fading
With each new year

What is art
Where do I start

It is yours
If you can find the time

It is yours
And
It is on your side

23 March 2015

Art

An idea
That works

To educate
And benefit us all

Now that is art

Do not sell yourself

Be yourself

Round A Corner

No one is ignoring you
No one does not love you
No one does not care

It hurt so much
They had to turn you off

If you could only show them

You want to

Get a little bit better

They will all be there

We will all be there

Winter Night 2015 (11:45pm)

Know It All

I felt like I was done learning
I felt like there was no inspiration in this world

So it turns out

I did not know anything at all

Dear April, No Rain. Dear April, Where Is May?

Today I will try
To say what I mean
To remember
What I said

To be firm
With my words
My heart soft
Use my head

I will keep up
With my family
I will call
An old friend

I will eat
What feels right
I will start
To live my life

For the very
First time
I start to breathe
I am alright

7 April 2015

Recurring Chorus

Composed and gracious
Save us sound

Composed and gracious
Save us now

15 April 2015

Translation

Natural high
From her eyes

She is just a drug

You should take it

Here is the drug

The TV said take it

The commercial

I hate it

There are no words
To describe

How a feeling is
Translated

This conversation
Is dated

Back to the start
Until forever

Or however far?
Whatever.

Use your mind
Choose your heart

Now restart

Write it down

Take my time
Use my heart

Take your mind
Create some art

16 April 2015

Let Life

Let life be interesting

Let life be fun

Learn from it all

Let life.

Be love.

Statistics

This group
That group
This sample
Take another sample?

Any way they have looked at it
The best way to lead

Is still by example

Untitled

It is either about love
The unknown
Or nothing at all

Nobody

My body
No body
Your body

What?

My body
Her body
Do not let me

Stop.

My body
Our body
Melt into

One

My body
Your body
We rise for the

Sun

Our body

Our body

This should be too
Fun

No body
Some body
I think I want

Love.

Green Aventurine

The scene
So green

The theme
So green

My Aventurine
Please

Well, if you'd like
Follow me

Because

Love
Plus
Love
Is always going to equal

Peace

Ah yes
Thank you

Now I see

Untitled II

As the beauty infiltrates
The pain will look for an escape

Amazing

To live
In a world
Where
There is
A setting
To redirect me
Into the
Right direction

I understand
For the
First time
That
Everything
Is amazing
And
Nothing
Is overwhelming

The weather will never
Phase me
I pray that my love
Will embrace me

Don't wake me

Please

Do not wake me
Stay with me
Save me

Spring Evening 2015 (10:56pm)

Before You Waste Another Second Of Our Time

I need direction

Not

Another lesson

Write it down

Lock it in

Okay

Now if you would like

You may begin

Spring 2015

Momentum

Can I get a little nudge
A little git up
Maybe a little emotion
Then some momentum
In the right direction
And I promise you
I will not trouble you
Anymore

Until tomorrow

April 2015 (4:46pm)

Live

I will fully enjoy the song
From now on

I will fully enjoy this song
From this day moving forward

I will not relate it to a memory
The color of sound is all I will see

The weights on my neck
The knots in my shoulders
The scars in my nerves
All of my muscles on fire

It is time to heal
Let the pain be

Please I beg
Just not on me

Spring 2015 (11:58pm)

Math

Direct Relationship
Thought versus pain
Motivation versus fear

No one ever told me
Love Road.
Turns
Right
Into
Insane

Get out of that lane

Please God
Cool down
My Brain.

Please God
Why do I
Have to wait?

Please God
Tell me the truth
About hate?

Will they judge?

Will they blame?

Is it true
That deep down
Inside
We are all the same?

Please God
How can I
Keep me

I mean
Us
Safe?

Slow it down
It is okay

Do us all a favor and stay.
Stay.
Stay.

Stay

Write It Down

I let go of any burdens that are not my own

I have ceased judgment
I refrain from negativity

Temporarily

Left

My mind

To find

My heart

April 2015

Recurring Thought

Still thinking about

Love

Love

Love

It's been so long

Love

Love

Love

I don't think I can

Love

Love

Love

Why won't you come to me

Love

Love

Love

Maybe I will get just one night of sleep

Love

Love

Love

No one taught me what is

Love

Love

Love

All the wrong people try to follow me

Love

Love

Love

When nobody is left on the streets

Love

Love

Love

I never said I was thinking these things

Love

Love

Love

I was trying to relay the wrong messages

Love

Love

Love

I was so tired sick weak

Love

Love

Love

But now I think I'm in

Love

Love

Love

Repeat...

21 April 2015 (3.22pm)

Hold On (Lyrics)

Hold on to the riverside

Another kid's gone and lost their mind

Please keep love and the river within sight

And in the morning we can go back home

In the morning we can go back...

Hold on to the riverside

Another kid thinks they're out of time

Please keep us and the river in the light

(Stay with me
I swear I'll never lie)

And in the morning we can go back home

Yes in the morning we can go back home

You may have prayed but I was so alone.

I don't pray much could you say one for me?

2 May 2015 (1:00am)

Restart

The only thing I worry about is worry itself

Remove the nerves that live deep in my gut

Release the tight grip that wraps around my heart

Input rejected?

Fuck that

Restart.

Control

Alt

Wait a minute.

Do not

Delete.

This may be art

Conjunction Gumption

There is no pressure

There is no worry

Ease my mind

I need to breathe on my own

I will focus on what is in front of me

I will not overthink the process

I will not waste my time with concern

For all I know

Is what I think

May be worse

Could very well

End up being

The best thing in the world

26 may 2015 (10:37pm)

It Is Hot. Damn.

The wind leaks through the holes in my skin
The air keeps me light
Please keep the natural light coming in

It is a good thing
It is a good thing

The water I drink never ceases to amaze
It keeps me happy
And completely free from the clouds and haze

You see?

The shower of love starts to fall from above
I do not need this hat
I do not need these clothes

Take them off

Hot damn
The concerns of worry
And the worry of fear
While trying to be a man

Turn it off

It is hot
Damn
How many times are you going to blame me when I believe this was your plan

Shake it off

Hot damn
The series of trials that have resulted in error
Are piled up in the back yard
With an old grill
A can of cola
Some old clothes
And a few of my own old phobias

Light them up
Let them burn
Then sweep them away

Dear Journal
Today I will be the best person I can be today

Nothing left to say

22 June 2015

Ground Me

I am likable.

I am at peace.

I am lovable.

I am stress free.

June 2015

•Resolution

I need to be modest.
I need to be mature.
I need to be relieved
Of this underlying feeling

That
Everything
I do

Is wrong.

Summer; Twenty Fifteen

I pray to god
To meditate
This time
Instead to see
What I need
Anxiety
And stress relief
For better days
And to feel free
For someone to
Maybe
Understand me
To breathe a little lighter
To feel the reflection
Of the sun
Off the sea
To soak in the salt
And float on top of the waves
Rushing towards me
And a beautiful dream
Of what is to be
And a restful night
With some peaceful sleep

1 August 2015 (8:15pm)

The Second; Time

There is only one thing
I notice

As I age
I am more focused

My single complaint

It is getting harder and harder
To blow my mind

With the same thing
2 times

Every

Day

Attempt at a Mantra (For Stress)

I will eat less.
I will need less.
I will not fear over your stress.
I will heal with time.
I will always be my best.

I will eat less.
I will need less.
I respect your opinion.
But
I must love myself.
And respect the practice.

I will eat less.
I will need less.
Grow with each day.
All I know is patience.
Forget the rest.

25 August 2015

Didn't It?

Her smile

contagious

Sensory

memory

seems to be

too much for me

It is not

how it seems

It is just

how we see it

Why can you

not believe it

I mean

The tree came from

A seed

Didn't it?

Repeat After Me

anxiety free.

heartburn free.

worry free.

stress free.

aware.

mindful of others.

mindful of me.

compassionate.

focused,

rested.

calm.

hopeful.

faithful.

grateful.

thankful.

relaxed.

and always

Unbreakable

3 September 2015

The Written Word

Your word

Is life

Your word

Is real

Your word's

No joke

Your word's

What you feel

Your words

Pick wise

Your word

Is time

Your word

Is light

Your words

Not mine

Your words

Impressions

Your words

Recollections

Your words

May have just been a joke

But now all the kids are drunk

And all the kids smoke

And all the kids are money hungry

All the kids think life is a hoax

Your words

Inspire

Your words

Reflect

Your words

Were the truth

And they have yet to impress

4 September 2015 (10:12pm)

Contradiction

Please
Relax

Breathe

I will not blame
I have no hate

In the end
I will love you

All the same

This was
Only
My opinion
On your
Recurring
Contradiction

Maybe in the future
We will both learn to listen

Little Little Light

A little little light

A little love

A little time

A little little hope

A little life

This little rhyme

A little little faith

A little scarred

A little hate

A little little feeling

A little thought

I will be okay

A little little light

A little breath

A little mile

A little little fear

A little heart

A little smile

A little little song

A little dream

A little night

A little little sleep

A little scared

But I will be alright

30 September 2015

Precipitation

Art is
Vain

No.

Art is
Rain

You cannot see it going up
However
You cannot miss the flood

Every once in a while
I still feel misunderstood

But
Uh
Umm
Ugh

Overall
I think
I am
Good.

September 2015

Mantra III

I can
I am
I'm me

Live
Dream
Repeat

This Is My Brave

Another thought
It is four am
How many hours left
Until I have to make myself face a day again

I think about yesterday
I think about tomorrow
I think about the future
All I think about is sorrow

So I wish for a little luck
For a love that
Shares my trust
For a key to let me in

There is no end
When will this end
You are not my friend
You are in my head

...and you are my only friend

So I shatter into glass
I am such a mess
I can never rest
All of my dreams end abruptly
And I wake up in a pool of stress

I will not ever hate

I will be gracious
I want to live
I want to see
I need to feel
I need to taste

It is a real disease
And it is of my brain

Shh…

I can make it back
It is not too late
I am resilient and determined
Just wait

I will love again
Someone
Will know my name

Breathe
It is okay
We are all just a person
We all feel just the same

I need to dissipate this negativity
I cannot wake up in fear of the rain
I am thinking

Way

Too

Fast

Again

Thank God
Those were the answers I think I once sought
But I really have to say I could do without all of this thought

Just write it out
Just write straight up
From negative to positive
And

Do

Not

Ever

Stop

The opposite of what you did to bury yourself under this rock

I hope I can be a better friend
I wish I could trust myself again
I hope this first good day never ends

I pray for silence in the bed I lay
I wish one person would understand me

I have trust in us all
That we will
Get up
After this fall

And that you too feel the same
I pray every night with the space for our names

I know with each day
We will add another
To the brave

Written July 2015; Performed 4 October 2015 Kaye Playhouse New York City (This Is My Brave NYC show)

Mantra IV

Stop saying I need
Start saying I can

Stop saying I wish
Start saying I am

Conclusion (Introduction)

I will not only be in love with the idea of things

I will be in love with doing them

Another Girl

I will never be jealous.

I will never be attached.

Weakness will make you crazy.

Make certain this lesson lasts.

There are

4

Billion

Women

In the

Whole

Wide

World

I think I can find someone

Damn

I promise there are other girls

10 October 2015

In My World

The news is not happening
In my world

The hate is not happening
In my world

The movies are not playing
In my world

The radio plays different songs

I do not have to stay up all night long

The TV show is just a mockery
Of what we need society to be

The game no one is playing
That is my world

The rich are not reigning
In my world

The reality star never happened
In my world

Tears are the only things streaming

And our chipped, off-white teeth are what is gleaming

Everything is not always what it is seeming

I want to know if you are okay

In my world

I just want you to care the same about me

In my world

I think I want to be
So please

One day you will
Maybe you'll see

Things are a little easier
In my world

I would love to meet you one day

In my world

10 October 2015 (11:12am)

Dropout

Some speak riddles
Some speak rumors
Some speak lies

Some speak with a false part of their mind

They do not even realize they

Divide us

When their real intention was to

Remind us

Must have read too many magazines

Text Books

A literal infusion of

Introductions

Bodies

Themes

Conclusions

And hooks

For the next book

Sometimes for the sake of my last 12 years

All the money I owe

All the women I lost

All the time I let go

I wish I had maybe given it a look

Not enough beautiful music
And could not completely feel the professors lessons

Pretentious
Protect us
Infectious
Redirect us

Some speak truth
That they have proven
Over time
With repetition
And social testing
Via both sides

Those tend to be the quotes
That I pass on and like

Those tend to be the only classes that my brain does not fight

A class
About positivity
And a candle
We ignite
The answer to the final exam

A light

Perfect
4 point 0
A plus

You may graduate

You were right the whole time

14 October 2015

Yesterday Today

I think

At one time

I spoke too much
About
The other side
Flowing faster
Through my mind
I am out of time
The tide
The tide
Has taken their side
I am all out of pride
I cannot breathe
I have given up

But giving up
Is not giving at all
It is taking a little piece
Away from everyone

I am done speaking
I have had enough
I need to sleep at night
I need to catch one sun
rise

Everyone is watching
But no one can see

I try to think of you
But narcissistically
I keep thinking of me

The rain
The lake
Catches all of us
Slides us into the stream
It keeps rolling faster
Throws me away from you
Into the endless sea

I won't say another word
I will not think another line
It was never about the things I would do
It was about how scared I was

That I was out of time

And in my mind
I had not done a thing
I had lost everything
Or maybe I gave it away
Because I could not see me deserving anything

Another bottle was
Not enough
My faith won again
Isn't that luck

Better breathe deep
Before the wave falls
From the sky
And sinks us all

But I can never drown
I can stand at any length
My hope for life
My need
My strength

I am running out of
Words each day

I need you love
I wish you would stay

I need you love
Yesterday

13 October 2015 (7:00pm)

One II

If one person
Relates to one line
Relates to the hard times
Relates to my overdriven

State of mind

I am out of time
I was over the line
All the blame is mine
But now we are on

The same side

City wide
State wide
Country wide
World wide

We have gotten so far
Now we ask for
The ability
To have a little pride

And maybe

Just maybe

No wait

Definabsofuckinglutely

For your genuine blessing

And

For the pain to subside

7 October 2015 (1:16pm)

Mantra XII

Be calm

Be honest

Be kind

Be aware

Be thoughtful

Show concern

Do not worry

Have care

Send positive vibrations out to the world
Then suck in all of the beautiful air

...Breathe...
...Repeat...
...Breathe...
...Repeat...

Trust me kid

Life wants to be fair

9 September 2015 (6pm)

Autumn Breeze

Simplify everything

All those thoughts

All those ideas

All the confusion

Down to the fact

That anything is possible

Why believe those illusions

Start with good

Start with hope

Come back to the ground

Regain focus

Get control of your thoughts

Clean them all up

Now try to use them

A Sunny Autumn Afternoon 2015 (2:02pm)

Dear Moon,

I am not needy
I am ready
I am driven
I have these gifts
And I must release them

I would love your support
I would love your guidance
I would love to share
The love
You have given

Please understand I have been patient
I think it is time we both stopped waiting

Please dream in sync with me from here on
And we can give these gifts until we are done

26 October (6:50pm)

Home

And I repeat!
One more time
This is the end of this show

Did you read this
They saved her
They pumped her veins
Full of love
Then was able to manage
All of her irrational
Thoughts of complacence
I cannot believe it took so long
In my deepest of hearts
I thought for sure
She had carried on too far about
Coincidences
And stars
About the
Road named Life
Stretching way too far
She finally broke down and cried
Prayed for something
Somebody
Someone
to give her some advice to
Reprogram her mind

Insert a little beauty
In her eyes to
Take up some permanent space
In the areas
That had been blind
What happened to all of my friends
What happened to my amazing family
What happened to all of this time
I want nothing more than to have back the last ten years of my life

Unfortunately those hours are gone
However there is some good news

Take a deep breath
Click your heals
Say gratitude

And your time in the real world
Will resume

27 October 2015 (11:21am)

Reaffirm

Breathe. Patience. Hope. Trust. Friends. Faith. Family. Love. Peace. Peace. Peace. It is okay to be yourself. It is okay to be myself. There are so many people in the world just like me. I can help. I am alright. I can heal myself. I can help others. Peace. Compassion. Kindness. I will find my way out of the darkness. I will take deep breaths when I am scared. I will take deep breaths when I am angry. I will take deep breaths before I make important decisions. I will call an old friend. I am sorry. I was in pain. I was confused. I was upset with myself, not you. Hope. Faith is not a religion. Positive affirmations. Growth. Compliment somebody. Get it in return. The definition of faith is trust. Patience. We can have faith in so many things. Ask the Universe for help. Meditate. Pray. Feel the change of season. Take a deep breath every morning when you wake. Gratitude. Be grateful. Breathe. It is okay to be happy. We all deserve happiness. We all deserve happiness. The air is here for everyone. Positivity. The sunlight is a disinfectant. The sun cleanses. The rain cleanses. All of this beauty. Organic growth. Kindness. Self-Compassion. Gratitude. Give light. Get light. Give hope. Get hope. Give peace. Get peace. Give love. Get love. Patience. Patience. Patience. Kindness grows. Grow. Do not be scared. Peace. Grow.

Be happy with yourself, and you cannot feel alone. Breathe. Gratitude. Thank you. -joe

15 November 2015

Christmas List 2015:

More love

Less stuff

27 November 2015 (11:17pm)

Untangled Thoughts

I am what I do

I am not what I think

For what I do

Is what I am

And my thoughts just

Create the plan

They cannot make me mad

They cannot get me sad

They ever so simply

Just weed out the bad

And my heart

Will explain exactly

Who I am

I promise you this

One day

You will understand

28 November 2015 (1pm)

What an amazing feeling. When we finally realize someone cares. It was always there. Sometimes you just have to ask for it.

Thank you to everyone that gave me another chance at being family. Thank you to everyone that gave me another chance at being a friend. Thank you to all the new inspirations in my life.

To a peaceful and love filled future.

I give up

I give up

It is over

The World

The Universe

The Force which is greater than I

Wins

And what do you know

Now we are all best friends.

The End

Made in the USA
Middletown, DE
20 November 2021

52366183R00109